Subtraction

This book belongs to

Sophie

FS109036 Subtraction

The Neighborhood

A fact family lives in each house. Use the fact families to subtract.

$5 + 1 = 6$ $4 + 2 = 6$ $3 + 1 = 4$

$1 + 5 = 6$ $2 + 4 = 6$ $1 + 3 = 4$

$6 - 1 =$ _____ $6 - 2 =$ _____ $4 - 1 =$ _____

$6 - 5 =$ _____ $6 - 4 =$ _____ $4 - 3 =$ _____

$3 + 2 = 5$ $2 + 1 = 3$ $4 + 1 = 5$

$2 + 3 = 5$ $1 + 2 = 3$ $1 + 4 = 5$

$5 - 2 =$ _____ $3 - 1 =$ _____ $5 - 1 =$ _____

$5 - 3 =$ _____ $3 - 2 =$ _____ $5 - 4 =$ _____

$2 + 2 = 4$ $5 + 0 = 5$ $3 + 3 = 6$

$4 - 2 =$ _____ $5 - 5 =$ _____ $6 - 3 =$ _____

FS109036 Subtraction

Car Fun

Add. Use the differences to answer the riddle.

What kind of song do you sing in a car?

___ ___ ___ ___ ___ ___ ___ ___ ___!
4   2   4   6   1   0   5   3

A

$6 - 2 =$ _____

T

$6 - 5 =$ _____

U

$5 - 5 =$ _____

C

$4 - 2 =$ _____

N

$5 - 0 =$ _____

E

$6 - 3 =$ _____

R

$6 - 0 =$ _____

3
reproducible

FS109036 Subtraction

Name _____

Boxcars

Find the differences.

$6 - 1 = \boxed{} - 2 = \boxed{} - 1 = \boxed{}$

$6 - 2 = \boxed{} - 1 = \boxed{} - 0 = \boxed{}$

$4 - 0 = \boxed{} - 2 = \boxed{} - 1 = \boxed{}$

$5 - 1 = \boxed{} - 1 = \boxed{} - 3 = \boxed{}$

FS109036 Subtraction

Name _____

Sailing Away

Subtract.

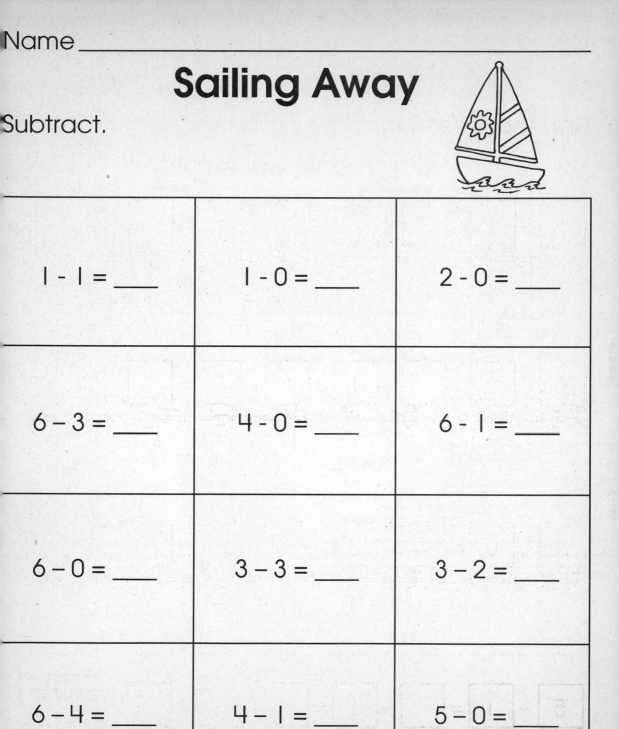

1 - 1 = ___	1 - 0 = ___	2 - 0 = ___
6 – 3 = ___	4 - 0 = ___	6 - 1 = ___
6 – 0 = ___	3 – 3 = ___	3 – 2 = ___
6 – 4 = ___	4 – 1 = ___	5 – 0 = ___

FS109036 Subtraction

Getting Around in Town

Use information from the graph to find the answers.

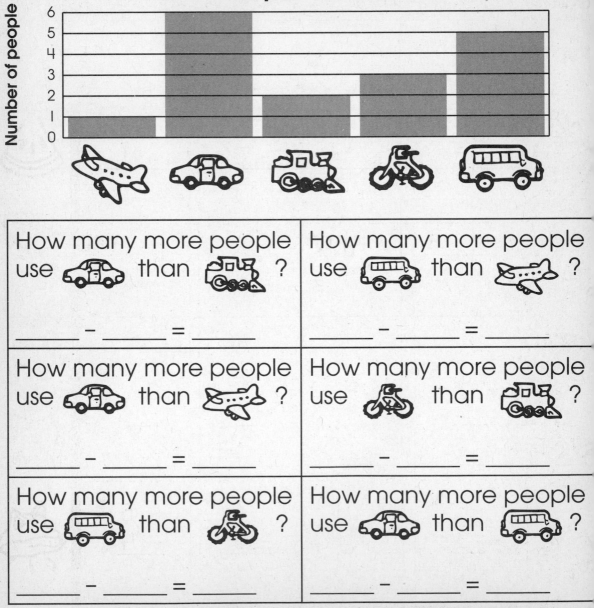

How People Get Around

How many more people use 🚗 than 🚂 ?

____ – ____ = ____

How many more people use 🚌 than ✈ ?

____ – ____ = ____

How many more people use 🚗 than ✈ ?

____ – ____ = ____

How many more people use 🚲 than 🚂 ?

____ – ____ = ____

How many more people use 🚌 than 🚲 ?

____ – ____ = ____

How many more people use 🚗 than 🚌 ?

____ – ____ = ____

Name _____

I Spy Something Red

To find out what I spy, color the boxes with differences of 1, 2, or 3. Then write the letters from the colored boxes in the blanks, working from left to right.

I spy a ___ ___ ___ ___ ___ ___ ___!

$6 - 2$ **K**	$4 - 3$ **C**	$5 - 3$ **A**	$6 - 1$ **T**
$5 - 2$ **B**	$4 - 2$ **O**	$5 - 1$ **L**	$6 - 2$ **R**
$4 - 0$ **S**	$6 - 0$ **U**	$3 - 2$ **O**	$5 - 1$ **W**
$5 - 0$ **M**	$4 - 0$ **B**	$6 - 3$ **S**	$5 - 4$ **E**

FS109036 Subtraction

Name _____

What's the Weather?

Use the fact families to subtract.

$1 + 6 = 7$

$6 + 1 = 7$

$7 - 1 = \underline{}$

$7 - 6 = \underline{}$

$2 + 5 = 7$

$5 + 2 = 7$

$7 - 2 = \underline{}$

$7 - 5 = \underline{}$

$3 + 4 = 7$

$4 + 3 = 7$

$7 - 4 = \underline{}$

$7 - 3 = \underline{}$

$2 + 6 = 8$

$6 + 2 = 8$

$8 - 2 = \underline{}$

$8 - 6 = \underline{}$

$3 + 5 = 8$

$5 + 3 = 8$

$8 - 3 = \underline{}$

$8 - 5 = \underline{}$

$4 + 4 = 8$

$8 - 4 = \underline{}$

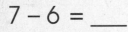

reproducible

FS109036 Subtraction

Name _____

Chilly!

Subtract. Use the differences to answer the riddle.

What did the snowman win at the Olympics?

$$\frac{\quad}{6} \qquad \frac{\quad}{4} \; \frac{\quad}{7} \; \frac{\quad}{2} \; \frac{\quad}{5}$$

$$\frac{\quad}{1} \; \frac{\quad}{3} \; \frac{\quad}{5} \; \frac{\quad}{6} \; \frac{\quad}{2} \; !$$

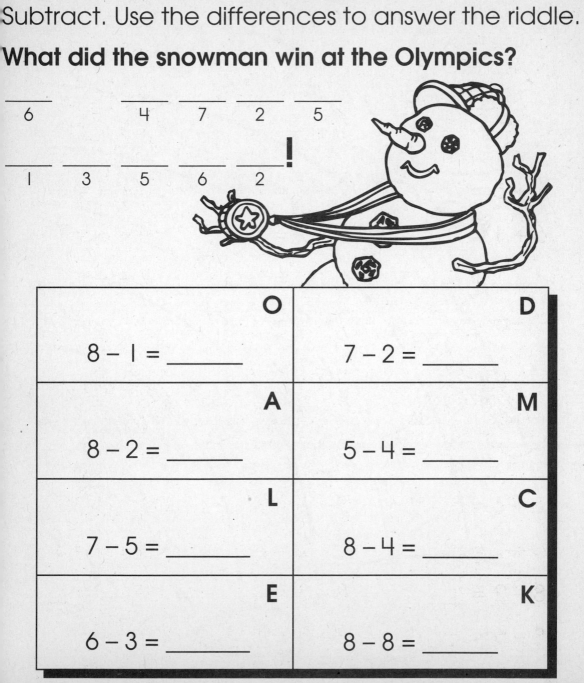

	O		D
	8 − 1 = _____		7 − 2 = _____

	A		M
	8 − 2 = _____		5 − 4 = _____

	L		C
	7 − 5 = _____		8 − 4 = _____

	E		K
	6 − 3 = _____		8 − 8 = _____

FS109036 Subtraction

Sun and Rain!

Find the differences to complete the paths through the rainbow.

$\square - 1 = \square$

$\square - 0 = \square$

$\square - 3 = \square$

$\square - 2 = \square$

$\square - 2 = \square$

$\square - 1 = \square$

$\square - 1 = \square$

$\square - 2 = \square$

$\square - 2 = \square$

$\square - 1 = \square$

$\square - 2 = \square$

$\square - 1 = \square$

$8 - 2 = \square$

$7 - 1 = \square$

$8 - 1 = \square$

$7 - 2 = \square$

$\square = \square$

FS109036 Subtraction

Weather Report: Snowy

Subtract. Connect the dots in order from least to greatest to find the hidden picture.

Start • 5 − 5 = ☐

Start

4 − 3 = ☐   • 4 − 3 = ☐

6 − 4 = ☐   • 5 − 3 = ☐

5 − 2 = ☐   • 7 − 4 = ☐

7 − 3 = ☐   • 8 − 4 = ☐

                 • 6 − 1 = ☐

8 − 3 = ☐ •

7 − 1 = ☐ •   • 8 − 2 = ☐

FS109036 Subtraction

Name _____

Weather Chart

Use information from the graph to find the answers

This Month's Weather

rainy			
rainy 🌧	||||| ||
cloudy ☁	||||| ||
sunny ☀	||||| |||
windy 💨				
snowy ❄	||||

How many more days were 🌧 than 💨 ?

____ – ____ = ____

How many more days were ☁ than ❄ ?

____ – ____ = ____

How many more days were ☀ than 💨 ?

____ – ____ = ____

How many more days were ❄ than 💨 ?

____ – ____ = ____

How many more days were ☀ than ☁ ?

____ – ____ = ____

How many more days were ☀ than 🌧 ?

____ – ____ = ____

FS109036 Subtraction

I Spy Something Blue

To find out what I spy, color the boxes with differences of 4, 5, or 6. Then write the letters from the colored boxes in the blanks, working from left to right.

I spy an __ __ __ __ __ __ __ __ __ **!**

8 **C** − 5	6 **U** − 2	7 **K** − 4	8 **M** − 3
7 **B** − 3	6 **R** − 1	5 **P** − 3	6 **V** − 3
6 **R** − 4	8 **T** − 6	8 **E** − 4	7 **L** − 2
5 **S** − 4	8 **L** − 2	7 **W** − 5	7 **A** − 1

Name _____

Around Town

Use the fact families to subtract.

$2 + 7 = 9$ $3 + 6 = 9$ $4 + 5 = 9$

$7 + 2 = 9$ $6 + 3 = 9$ $5 + 4 = 9$

$9 - 2 = $ ___ $9 - 3 = $ ___ $9 - 5 = $ ___

$9 - 7 = $ ___ $9 - 6 = $ ___ $9 - 4 = $ ___

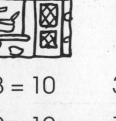
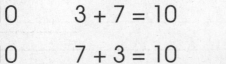

$2 + 8 = 10$ $3 + 7 = 10$ $4 + 6 = 10$

$8 + 2 = 10$ $7 + 3 = 10$ $6 + 4 = 10$ $5 + 5 = 10$

$10 - 2 = $ ___ $10 - 3 = $ ___ $10 - 4 = $ ___ $10 - 5 = $ ___

$10 - 8 = $ ___ $10 - 7 = $ ___ $10 - 6 = $ ___

FS109036 Subtraction

Name _____

Our Town

Subtract. Use the differences to answer the riddle.

What runs in and out of town all day and all night?

____ ____ ____ ____ ____ ____ ____ **!**
 2   6   3   4   7   7   3

	R		I
	$9 - 5 = $ _____		$10 - 2 = $ _____
	T		**A**
	$10 - 7 = $ _____		$10 - 8 = $ _____
	S		**H**
	$9 - 3 = $ _____		$9 - 4 = $ _____
	E		**Y**
	$9 - 2 = $ _____		$10 - 9 = $ _____

FS109036 Subtraction

Firemen's Ladders

Find the differences to complete the paths.
Start at the top.

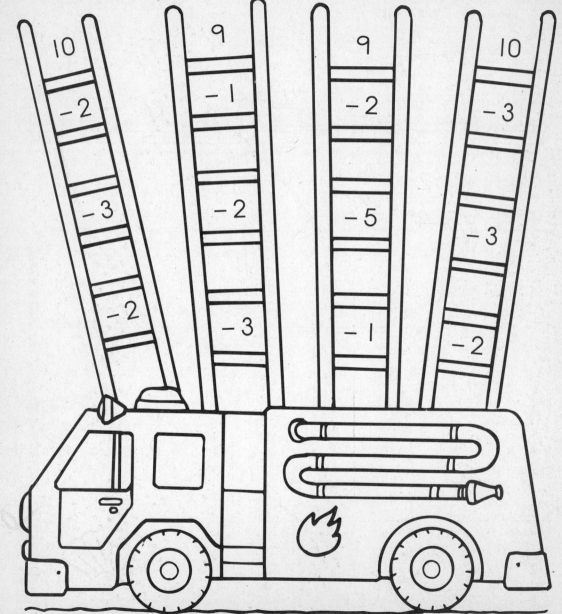

10
− 2
− 3
− 2

9
− 1
− 2
− 3

9
− 2
− 5
− 1

10
− 3
− 3
− 2

Space Walk

Subtract.

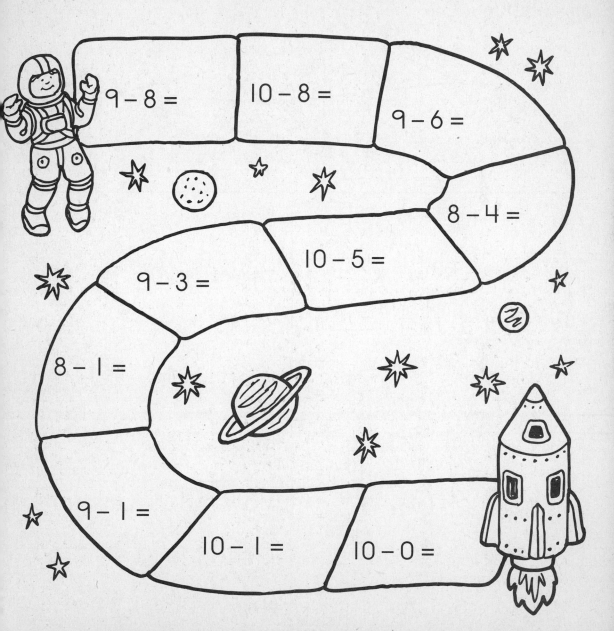

$9 - 8 =$

$10 - 8 =$

$9 - 6 =$

$8 - 4 =$

$10 - 5 =$

$9 - 3 =$

$8 - 1 =$

$9 - 1 =$

$10 - 1 =$

$10 - 0 =$

FS109036 Subtraction

Name _____

Town Map

Use information from the map to find the answer in miles.

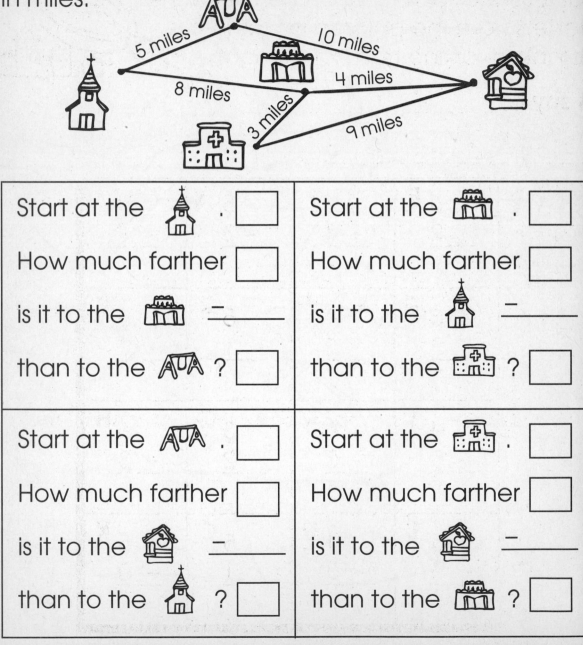

Start at the 🏛️ . ☐

How much farther ☐

is it to the 🏛️ — ____

than to the A∪A ? ☐

Start at the 🏛️ . ☐

How much farther ☐

is it to the 🏛️ — ____

than to the 🏥 ? ☐

Start at the A∪A . ☐

How much farther ☐

is it to the 🏠 — ____

than to the 🏛️ ? ☐

Start at the 🏥 . ☐

How much farther ☐

is it to the 🏠 — ____

than to the 🏛️ ? ☐

FS109036 Subtraction

Name _____

I Spy Something in Town

To find out what I spy, color the boxes with differences of 4, 5, or 6. Then write the letters from the colored boxes in the blanks, working from left to right.

I spy a ____ ____ ____

____ ____ ____ ____ ____!

6 **F** − 2	4 **P** − 3	5 **S** − 3	6 **I** − 1
5 **Q** − 2	4 **F** − 2	5 **R** − 1	6 **E** − 2
4 **T** − 0	6 **R** − 0	3 **G** − 2	6 **H** − 3
5 **L** − 4	4 **U** − 0	5 **C** − 1	5 **K** − 0

19
reproducible

FS109036 Subtraction

Number Garden

Use the fact families to subtract.

$2 + 9 = 11$	$3 + 8 = 11$	$4 + 7 = 11$	$5 + 6 = 11$
$9 + 2 = 11$	$8 + 3 = 11$	$7 + 4 = 11$	$6 + 5 = 11$
$11 - 2 = \underline{\quad}$	$11 - 3 = \underline{\quad}$	$11 - 4 = \underline{\quad}$	$11 - 6 = \underline{\quad}$
$11 - 9 = \underline{\quad}$	$11 - 8 = \underline{\quad}$	$11 - 7 = \underline{\quad}$	$11 - 5 = \underline{\quad}$

$3 + 9 = 12$	$4 + 8 = 12$	$5 + 7 = 12$	
$9 + 3 = 12$	$8 + 4 = 12$	$7 + 5 = 12$	$6 + 6 = 12$
$12 - 3 = \underline{\quad}$	$12 - 4 = \underline{\quad}$	$12 - 5 = \underline{\quad}$	$12 - 6 = \underline{\quad}$
$12 - 9 = \underline{\quad}$	$12 - 8 = \underline{\quad}$	$12 - 7 = \underline{\quad}$	

FS109036 Subtraction

Name _____

Duck Wear

Subtract. Use the differences to answer the riddle.

What kind of suit does a duck wear?

___ ___ ___ ___ ___ - ___ ___ ___ ___ ___ !
3   2   7   6   9   4   8   8   2   5

M	**U**	**O**
$12 - 1 =$ _____	$11 - 4 =$ _____	$11 - 6 =$ _____
C	**T**	**K**
$12 - 6 =$ _____	$12 - 0 =$ _____	$12 - 3 =$ _____
S	**R**	**P**
$12 - 8 =$ _____	$11 - 1 =$ _____	$9 - 8 =$ _____
A	**D**	**E**
$12 - 9 =$ _____	$10 - 8 =$ _____	$12 - 4 =$ _____

FS109036 Subtraction

Name _____

Fly the Coop!

Find the differences to complete the paths.
Start at the top and
go down.

FS109036 Subtraction

On the Farm

Subtract.

$$\begin{array}{r} 12 \\ -\ 9 \\ \hline \end{array}$$

$$\begin{array}{r} 10 \\ -\ 9 \\ \hline \end{array} \quad \begin{array}{r} 12 \\ -\ 7 \\ \hline \end{array} \quad \begin{array}{r} 9 \\ -\ 6 \\ \hline \end{array}$$

$$\begin{array}{r} 12 \\ -\ 2 \\ \hline \end{array} \quad \begin{array}{r} 10 \\ -\ 7 \\ \hline \end{array} \quad \begin{array}{r} 12 \\ -\ 5 \\ \hline \end{array}$$

$$\begin{array}{r} 11 \\ -\ 9 \\ \hline \end{array} \quad \begin{array}{r} 12 \\ -\ 8 \\ \hline \end{array} \quad \begin{array}{r} 11 \\ -\ 7 \\ \hline \end{array}$$

$$\begin{array}{r} 11 \\ -\ 4 \\ \hline \end{array} \quad \begin{array}{r} 9 \\ -\ 4 \\ \hline \end{array} \quad \begin{array}{r} 10 \\ -\ 3 \\ \hline \end{array} \quad \begin{array}{r} 11 \\ -\ 6 \\ \hline \end{array}$$

$$\begin{array}{r} 12 \\ -\ 6 \\ \hline \end{array} \quad \begin{array}{r} 10 \\ -\ 8 \\ \hline \end{array} \quad \begin{array}{r} 10 \\ -\ 5 \\ \hline \end{array}$$

$$\begin{array}{r} 10 \\ -\ 4 \\ \hline \end{array} \quad \begin{array}{r} 11 \\ -\ 8 \\ \hline \end{array} \quad \begin{array}{r} 12 \\ -\ 3 \\ \hline \end{array} \quad \begin{array}{r} 9 \\ -\ 5 \\ \hline \end{array}$$

FS109036 Subtraction

Name _____

Cows and Corn

Use information from the chart to find the answers.

Cow	Ears of Corn Eaten
Daisy	5
Clara	6
Gertie	5
Flora	7
Ida	4
Maizy	6

Clara had 11 ears of corn.

She ate _____

She has _____ left.

Maizy had 12 ears of corn.

She ate _____

She has _____ left.

Ida had 11 ears of corn.

She ate _____

She has _____ left.

Gertie had 12 ears of corn.

She ate _____

She has _____ left.

Flora had 10 ears of corn.

She ate _____

She has _____ left.

Daisy had 11 ears of corn.

She ate _____

She has _____ left.

FS109036 Subtraction

Name _____

I Spy Something Green

To find out what I spy, color the boxes with differences of 5, 6, or 7. Then write the letters from the colored boxes in the blanks, working from left to right.

I spy a ___ ___ ___ ___ ___ ___ ___ !

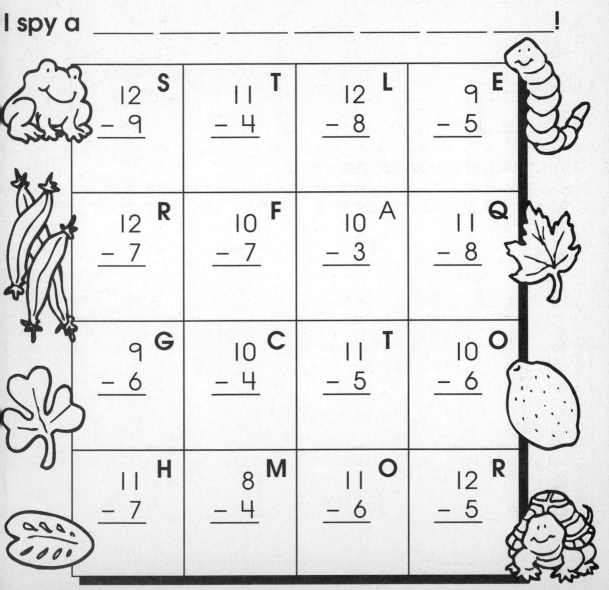

12 −9 **S**	11 −4 **T**	12 −8 **L**	9 −5 **E**
12 −7 **R**	10 −7 **F**	10 −3 **A**	11 −8 **Q**
9 −6 **G**	10 −4 **C**	11 −5 **T**	10 −6 **O**
11 −7 **H**	8 −4 **M**	11 −6 **O**	12 −5 **R**

Name _____

Sports

Use the fact families to subtract.

$4 + 9 = 13$

$9 + 4 = 13$

$13 - 4 = $ _____

$13 - 9 = $ _____

$5 + 8 = 13$

$8 + 5 = 13$

$13 - 5 = $ _____

$13 - 8 = $ _____

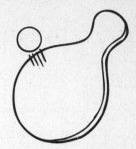

$6 + 7 = 13$

$7 + 6 = 13$

$13 - 6 = $ _____

$13 - 7 = $ _____

$5 + 9 = 14$

$9 + 5 = 14$

$14 - 5 = $ _____

$14 - 9 = $ _____

$6 + 8 = 14$

$8 + 6 = 14$

$14 - 6 = $ _____

$14 - 8 = $ _____

$7 + 7 = 14$

$14 - 7 = $ _____

FS109036 Subtraction

Batter Up!

Subtract. Use the differences to answer the riddle.

What did the mitt say to the baseball?

___ ___ ___ ___ ___
2   9   6   2   5

___ ___ ___   ___ ___ ___ ___ ___!
7   3 10   11 9 6 4 1

I	U	Y
$14 - 2 = $ _____	$11 - 1 = $ _____	$14 - 7 = $ _____
C	**H**	**O**
$10 - 8 = $ _____	$13 - 8 = $ _____	$12 - 9 = $ _____
E	**R**	**P**
$13 - 9 = $ _____	$9 - 8 = $ _____	$14 - 6 = $ _____
T	**A**	**L**
$13 - 7 = $ _____	$14 - 5 = $ _____	$12 - 1 = $ _____

FS109036 Subtraction

Name _____

Dunk It!

Find the differences to complete the paths. Start at the top and go down.

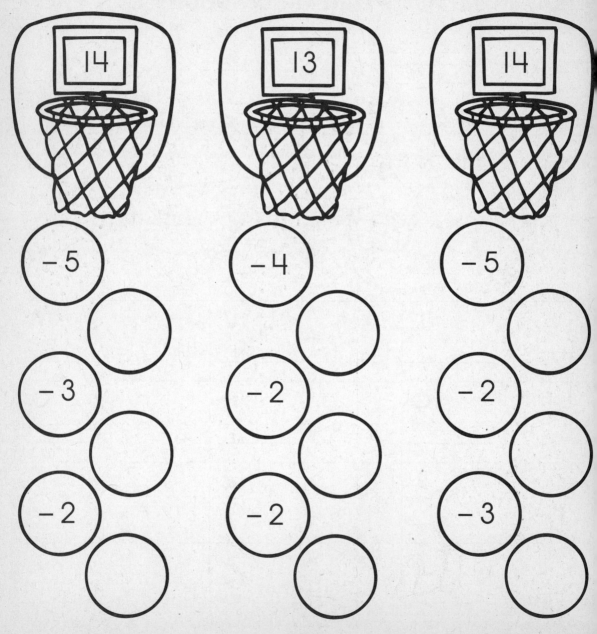

Preparation

Remove the game board and cards from the center of the book. Cut out the cards. Provide a game piece for each player and a die for the game.

How to Play

One child can play this game alone or two or more children can play. The children stack the cards facedown and put their game pieces on START. The first player draws a card and solves the subtraction problem on it. If he or she is correct, the player rolls the die and moves his or her game piece the number of spaces rolled. If he or she is incorrect, the player's turn is over. The next player takes a turn. The players check one another's answers. Play continues until someone wins by reaching FINISH. Some spaces have directions on them that the players must follow if they land on them. For a cooperative game, have the game end when all the players have reached FINISH. For more of a challenge, each player can also write on paper a different subtraction problem that has the same answer.

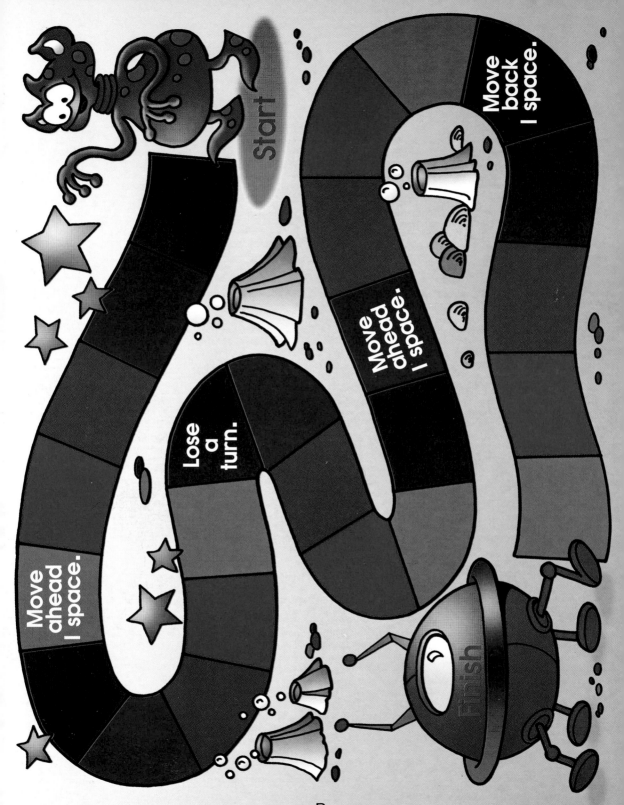

Start

Move back
1 space.

Move
ahead
1 space.

Lose
a
turn.

Move
ahead
1 space.

Finish

B

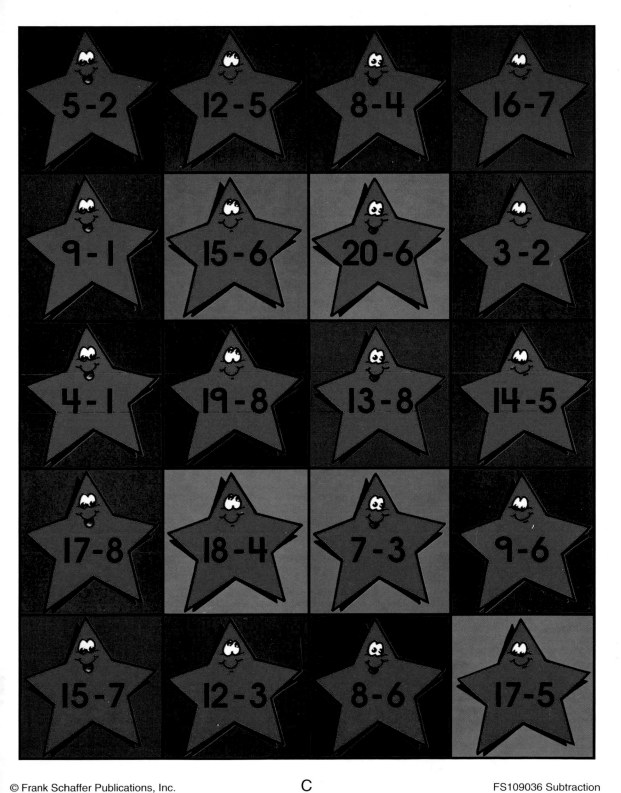

C

FS109036 Subtraction

D

Name _____

A Great Catch!

Subtract.

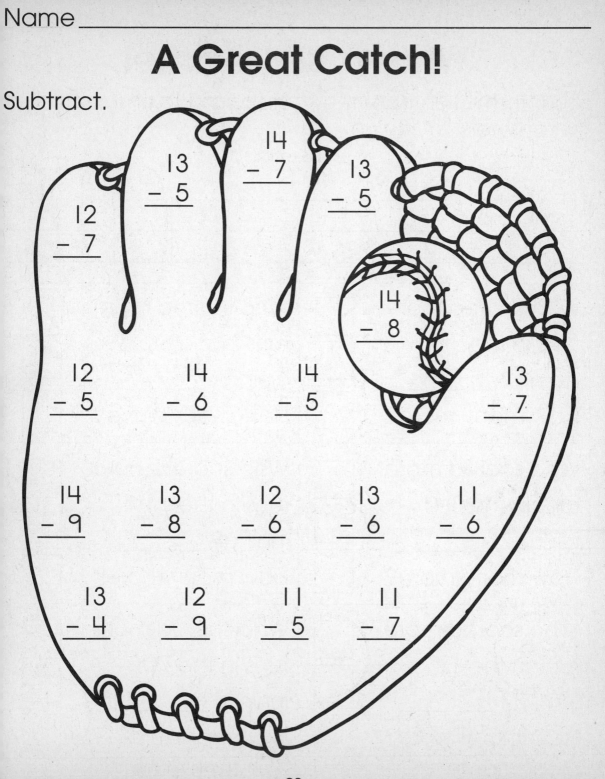

12
− 7
_____

13
− 5
_____

14
− 7
_____

13
− 5
_____

14
− 8
_____

12
− 5
_____

14
− 6
_____

14
− 5
_____

13
− 7
_____

14
− 9
_____

13
− 8
_____

12
− 6
_____

13
− 6
_____

11
− 6
_____

13
− 4
_____

12
− 9
_____

11
− 5
_____

11
− 7
_____

FS109036 Subtraction

What a Ball Game!

Use information from the scoreboard to find the answers.

Runs scored

Inning	1	2	3	4	5	6	7	8	9
Cubs	8	14	14	5	12	6	5	13	11
Reds	13	7	8	13	6	14	12	7	5

Who scored more runs in the 4th inning? _____

How many more?

☐ − ☐ ☐

Who scored more runs in the 8th inning? _____

How many more?

☐ − ☐ ☐

Who scored more runs in the 3rd inning? _____

How many more?

☐ − ☐ ☐

Who scored more runs in the 6th inning? _____

How many more?

☐ − ☐ ☐

Who scored more runs in the 1st inning? _____

How many more?

☐ − ☐ ☐

Who scored more runs in the 7th inning? _____

How many more?

☐ − ☐ ☐

FS109036 Subtraction

Name _____

I Spy Something Black

To find out what I spy, color the boxes with differences of 6, 7, or 8. Then write the letters from the colored boxes in the blanks, working from left to right.

I spy a ___ ___ ___ ___ ___ ___ ___ ___ ___ ___ ___ ___ ___!

12 L – 7	14 H – 8	13 S – 8	13 O – 6
12 C – 6	11 K – 4	14 P – 9	13 E – 7
14 Y – 7	11 T – 7	14 P – 6	11 R – 6
12 U – 4	14 Q – 5	13 C – 5	12 K – 5

FS109036 Subtraction

Name _____

Sailing

Use the fact families to subtract.

6 + 9 = 15	7 + 8 = 15	7 + 9 = 16	
9 + 6 = 15	8 + 7 = 15	9 + 7 = 16	8 + 8 = 16
15 − 6 = ___	15 − 7 = ___	16 − 7 = ___	16 − 8 = ___
15 − 9 = ___	15 − 8 = ___	16 − 9 = ___	

Practice.

16 − 9 = ___	14 − 9 = ___	16 − 8 = ___
15 − 6 = ___	12 − 6 = ___	15 − 7 = ___
11 − 2 = ___	11 − 5 = ___	11 − 9 = ___
16 − 7 = ___	13 − 7 = ___	15 − 9 = ___
15 − 8 = ___	12 − 8 = ___	13 − 8 = ___

FS109036 Subtraction

Name _____

What Big Teeth You Have!

Subtract. Use the differences to answer the riddle.

What do you get from an alligator in a bad mood?

___ ___ ___ ___   ___ ___ ___ ___!
5   7   8   7   9   7   6

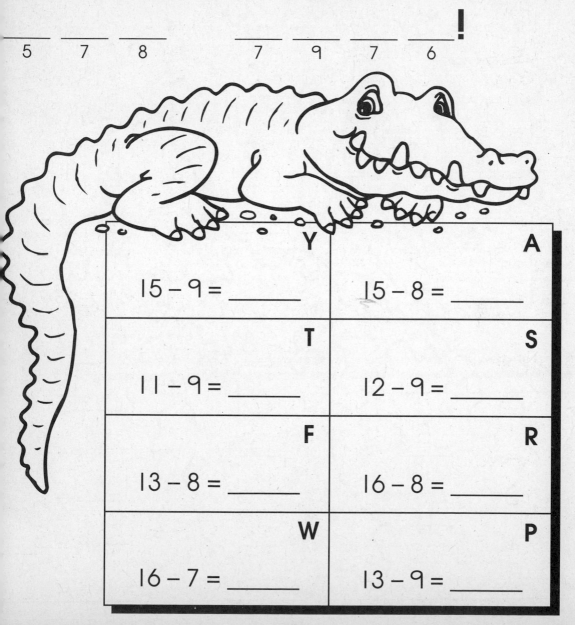

Y $15 - 9 =$ ___	**A** $15 - 8 =$ ___
T $11 - 9 =$ ___	**S** $12 - 9 =$ ___
F $13 - 8 =$ ___	**R** $16 - 8 =$ ___
W $16 - 7 =$ ___	**P** $13 - 9 =$ ___

FS109036 Subtraction

The Coral Reef

Find the differences to complete the paths. Start at the top and go down.

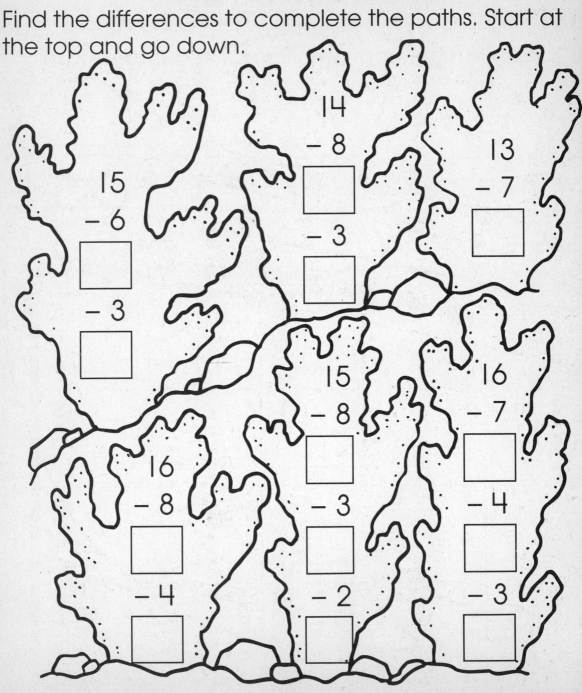

FS109036 Subtraction

Name _____

Ahoy There!

Subtract.

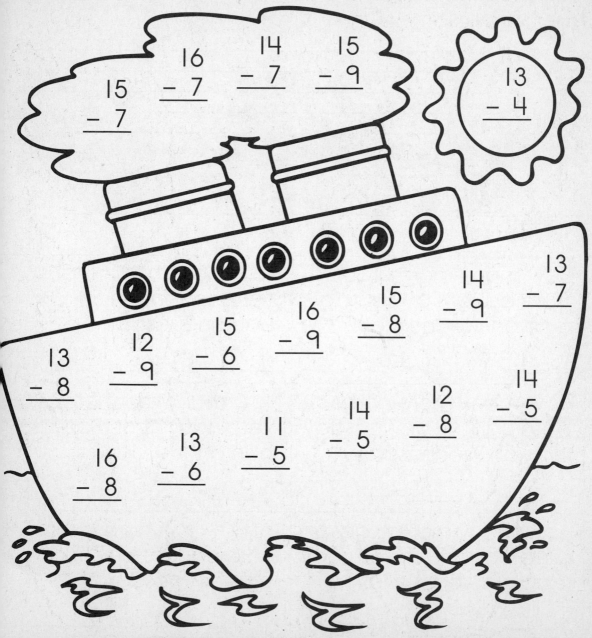

$$15 - 7$$

$$16 - 7$$

$$14 - 7$$

$$15 - 9$$

$$13 - 4$$

$$13 - 7$$

$$14 - 9$$

$$15 - 8$$

$$16 - 9$$

$$15 - 6$$

$$12 - 9$$

$$13 - 8$$

$$14 - 5$$

$$12 - 8$$

$$14 - 5$$

$$11 - 5$$

$$13 - 6$$

$$16 - 8$$

Name _____

Crab Catch

Use information in the bar graph to find the answers.

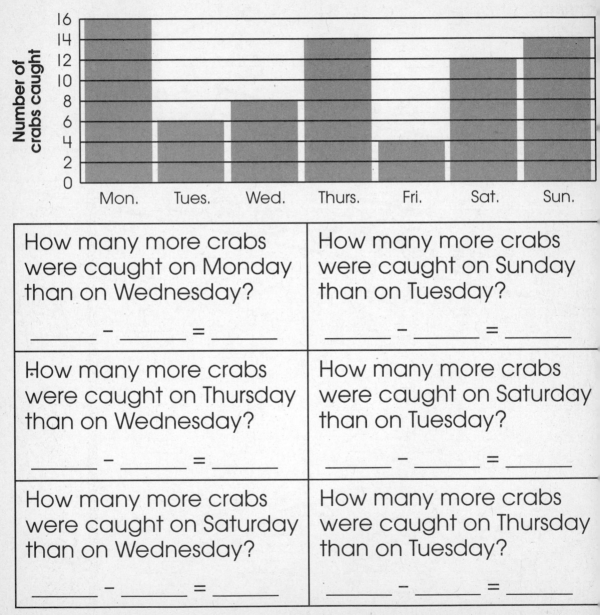

How many more crabs were caught on Monday than on Wednesday?	How many more crabs were caught on Sunday than on Tuesday?
_____ – _____ = _____	_____ – _____ = _____
How many more crabs were caught on Thursday than on Wednesday?	How many more crabs were caught on Saturday than on Tuesday?
_____ – _____ = _____	_____ – _____ = _____
How many more crabs were caught on Saturday than on Wednesday?	How many more crabs were caught on Thursday than on Tuesday?
_____ – _____ = _____	_____ – _____ = _____

Name _____

I Spy Something Shiny!

To find out what I spy, color the boxes with differences of 7, 8, or 9. Then write the letters from the colored boxes in the blanks, working from left to right.

I spy a ___ ___ ___ ___ ___ ___

___ ___ ___ ___ ___ ___ ___!

15 **P** − 7	16 **I** − 9	14 **L** − 8	14 **R** − 7
13 **A** − 6	12 **T** − 5	16 **E** − 8	13 **T** − 5
14 **R** − 6	14 **E** − 5	13 **T** − 8	15 **A** − 6
16 **S** − 7	12 **U** − 4	13 **R** − 4	15 **E** − 8

FS109036 Subtraction

Looking at the Seasons

Use the fact families to subtract.

$8 + 9 = 17$

$9 + 8 = 17$ $9 + 9 = 18$

$17 - 8 = $ _____ $18 - 9 = $ _____

$17 - 9 = $ _____

Practice.

$15 - 6 = $ _____ $13 - 6 = $ _____ $17 - 9 = $ _____

$11 - 5 = $ _____ $14 - 7 = $ _____ $15 - 8 = $ _____

$16 - 9 = $ _____ $17 - 8 = $ _____ $11 - 7 = $ _____

$16 - 7 = $ _____ $15 - 9 = $ _____ $16 - 8 = $ _____

$18 - 9 = $ _____ $15 - 7 = $ _____ $14 - 8 = $ _____

$17 - 8 = $ _____ $12 - 7 = $ _____ $14 - 9 = $ _____

Name _____

What a Fall!

Subtract. Use the differences to answer the riddle.

What falls often but never gets hurt?

___ ___ ___ ___ **!**
7   8   9   6

G	**O**
$12 - 8 =$ _____	$18 - 9 =$ _____
P	**L**
$14 - 9 =$ _____	$11 - 9 =$ _____
T	**S**
$12 - 9 =$ _____	$15 - 8 =$ _____
W	**N**
$13 - 7 =$ _____	$17 - 9 =$ _____

39
reproducible

FS109036 Subtraction

Leaves Are Falling

Find the differences to complete the paths.
Start at the top and go down.

Name _____

Summertime

Subtract.

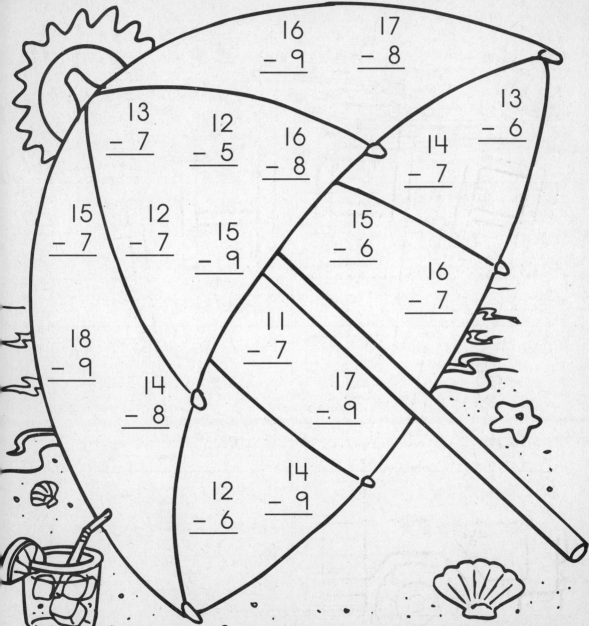

FS109036 Subtraction

Name _____

Hit the Slopes!

Use the prices to find the answers.

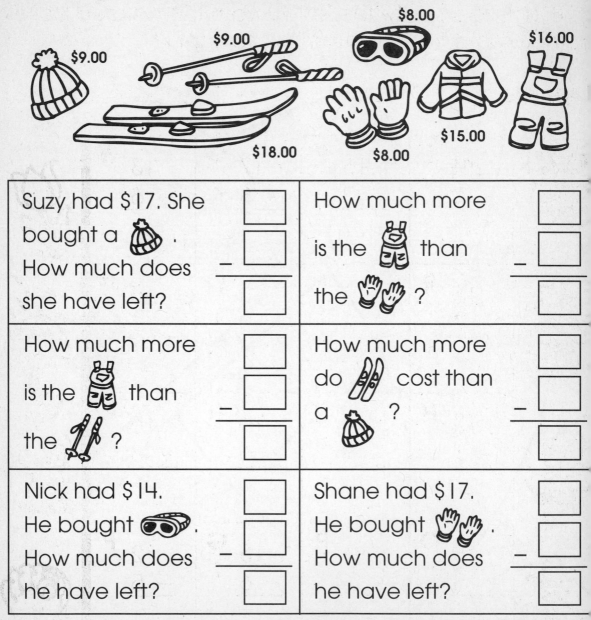

$9.00

$9.00

$8.00

$16.00

$18.00

$8.00

$15.00

Suzy had $17. She bought a 🧢. How much does she have left?	☐ –☐ ☐	How much more is the 👖 than the 🧤?	☐ –☐ ☐
How much more is the 👖 than the 🎿?	☐ –☐ ☐	How much more do 🎿 cost than a 🧢?	☐ –☐ ☐
Nick had $14. He bought 🥽. How much does he have left?	☐ –☐ ☐	Shane had $17. He bought 🧤. How much does he have left?	☐ –☐ ☐

42
reproducible

FS109036 Subtractio

Name _____

I Spy Something in the Spring

To find out what I spy, color the boxes with differences of 8 or 9. Then write the letters from the colored boxes in the blanks, working from left to right.

I spy a ____ ____ ____ ____ ____ ____ ____ ____ ____ !

14 − 7 **L**	16 − 9 **P**	17 − 8 **G**	13 − 6 **W**
16 − 7 **R**	15 − 8 **F**	18 − 9 **O**	15 − 7 **U**
13 − 7 **H**	17 − 9 **N**	14 − 6 **D**	16 − 8 **H**
18 − 9 **O**	14 − 7 **R**	15 − 6 **G**	12 − 5 **P**

FS109036 Subtraction

Name _____

House Numbers

Use all of the facts you know to subtract.

$$57 - 32$$

$$68 - 24$$

$$67 - 13$$

$$58 - 23$$

$$72 - 51$$

$$98 - 36$$

$$95 - 92$$

$$27 - 11$$

$$18 - 12$$

$$99 - 25$$

$$65 - 40$$

FS109036 Subtraction

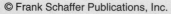

Out of This World

Subtract. Use the differences to answer the riddle.

What game do astronauts like to play?

__ __ __ __ __ __ __ __ __ !
53 36 36 82 36 27 36 41 60

P 38 − 11	**O** 59 − 23
R 96 − 71	**F** 88 − 17
M 96 − 43	**N** 93 − 11
L 77 − 36	**Y** 99 − 39

Name _____

Lift Off!

Subtract.

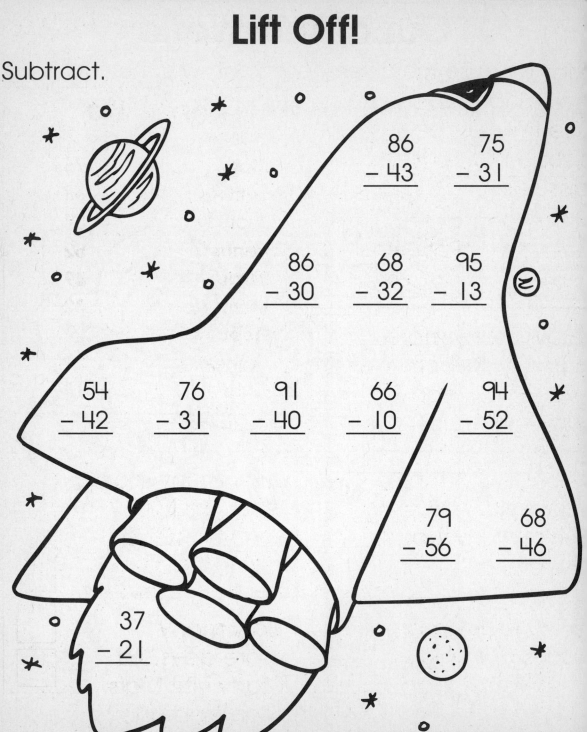

$$\begin{array}{r} 86 \\ -43 \\ \hline \end{array} \qquad \begin{array}{r} 75 \\ -31 \\ \hline \end{array}$$

$$\begin{array}{r} 86 \\ -30 \\ \hline \end{array} \qquad \begin{array}{r} 68 \\ -32 \\ \hline \end{array} \qquad \begin{array}{r} 95 \\ -13 \\ \hline \end{array}$$

$$\begin{array}{r} 54 \\ -42 \\ \hline \end{array} \quad \begin{array}{r} 76 \\ -31 \\ \hline \end{array} \quad \begin{array}{r} 91 \\ -40 \\ \hline \end{array} \quad \begin{array}{r} 66 \\ -10 \\ \hline \end{array} \quad \begin{array}{r} 94 \\ -52 \\ \hline \end{array}$$

$$\begin{array}{r} 79 \\ -56 \\ \hline \end{array} \qquad \begin{array}{r} 68 \\ -46 \\ \hline \end{array}$$

$$\begin{array}{r} 37 \\ -21 \\ \hline \end{array}$$

FS109036 Subtraction

Name _____

Space Travel

Marty has been traveling to the planets. Use the numbers in his space log to find the answers.

Space Log	
Planet	Days Visited
Mars	**76**
Earth	**68**
Jupiter	**57**
Venus	**52**
Saturn	**49**
Mercury	**32**
Neptune	**24**
Uranus	**21**
Pluto	**13**

How many more days did Marty visit Earth than Jupiter?
☐ − ☐ = ☐

How many more days did Marty visit Saturn than Neptune?
☐ − ☐ = ☐

How many more days did Marty visit Venus than Uranus?
☐ − ☐ = ☐

How many more days did Marty visit Venus than Mercury?
☐ − ☐ = ☐

How many more days did Marty visit Mars than Neptune?
☐ − ☐ = ☐

Name _____

I Spy Something Flying!

To find out what I spy, color the boxes with differences from 60 to 72. Then write the letters from the colored boxes in the blanks, working from left to right.

I spy a ____ ____ ____ ____ ____

____ ____ ____ ____ ____ ____ ____ ____ !

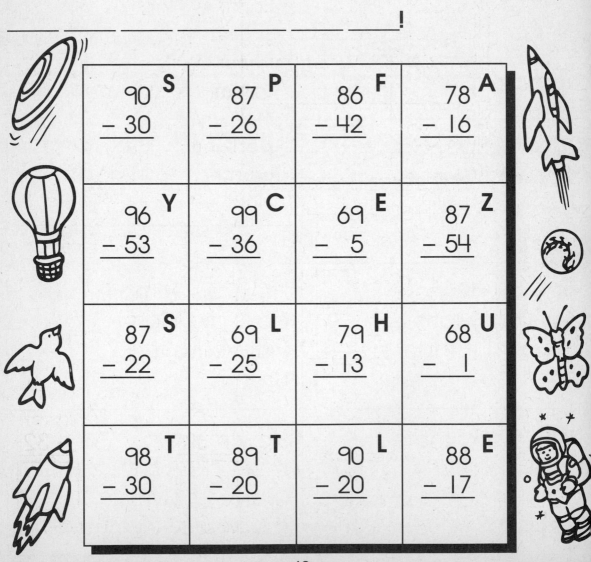

90 **S** − 30	87 **P** − 26	86 **F** − 42	78 **A** − 16
96 **Y** − 53	99 **C** − 36	69 **E** − 5	87 **Z** − 54
87 **S** − 22	69 **L** − 25	79 **H** − 13	68 **U** − 1
98 **T** − 30	89 **T** − 20	90 **L** − 20	88 **E** − 17

48
reproducible

FS109036 Subtractio

Name _____

Tic-Tac-Toe

Find the differences. Then mark X or O over the answers on the tic-tac-toe game to find the winner!

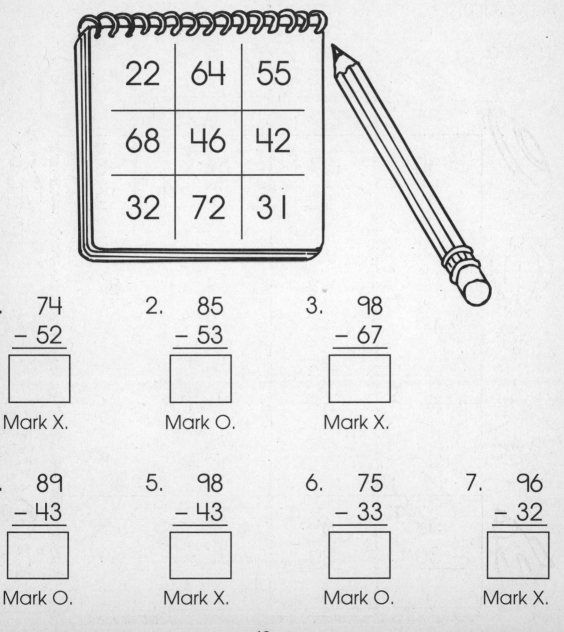

22	64	55
68	46	42
32	72	31

1.　74
　 − 52

Mark X.

2.　85
　 − 53

Mark O.

3.　98
　 − 67

Mark X.

4.　89
　 − 43

Mark O.

5.　98
　 − 43

Mark X.

6.　75
　 − 33

Mark O.

7.　96
　 − 32

Mark X.

Name _____

Bingo!

Find the differences. Color the answers on the Bingo cards. Be careful! Some answers are on both. The first board to be completely covered is the winner!

50	35	43
21	65	32

$$
\begin{array}{r} 86 \\ -\ 43 \end{array}
\qquad
\begin{array}{r} 92 \\ -\ 71 \end{array}
\qquad
\begin{array}{r} 85 \\ -\ 52 \end{array}
\qquad
\begin{array}{r} 76 \\ -\ 41 \end{array}
\qquad
\begin{array}{r} 67 \\ -\ 35 \end{array}
$$

$$
\begin{array}{r} 74 \\ -\ 30 \end{array}
\qquad
\begin{array}{r} 98 \\ -\ 33 \end{array}
\qquad
\begin{array}{r} 83 \\ -\ 60 \end{array}
\qquad
\begin{array}{r} 79 \\ -\ 38 \end{array}
$$

32	23	33
41	43	44

FS109036 Subtractio

Name _____

Go Fish!

Subtract.

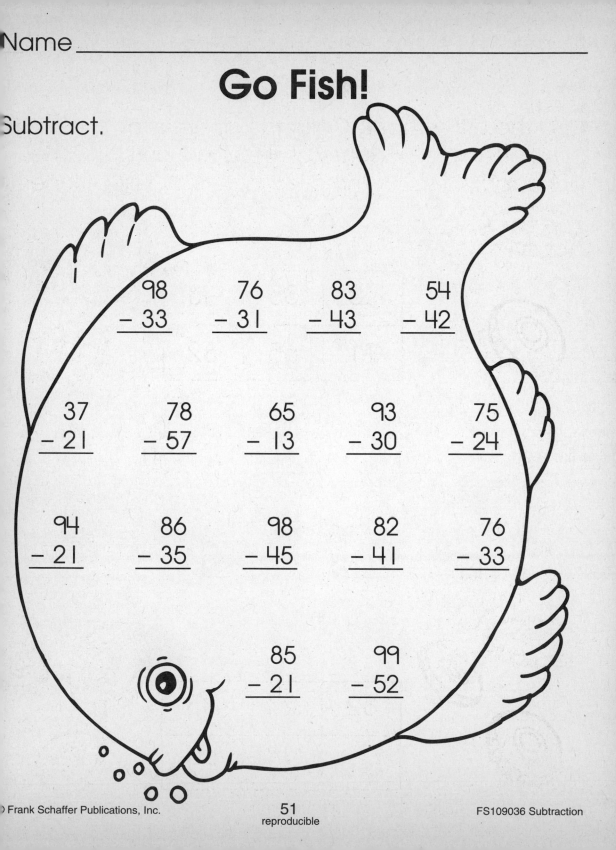

$$\begin{array}{r} 98 \\ -33 \\ \hline \end{array} \quad \begin{array}{r} 76 \\ -31 \\ \hline \end{array} \quad \begin{array}{r} 83 \\ -43 \\ \hline \end{array} \quad \begin{array}{r} 54 \\ -42 \\ \hline \end{array}$$

$$\begin{array}{r} 37 \\ -21 \\ \hline \end{array} \quad \begin{array}{r} 78 \\ -57 \\ \hline \end{array} \quad \begin{array}{r} 65 \\ -13 \\ \hline \end{array} \quad \begin{array}{r} 93 \\ -30 \\ \hline \end{array} \quad \begin{array}{r} 75 \\ -24 \\ \hline \end{array}$$

$$\begin{array}{r} 94 \\ -21 \\ \hline \end{array} \quad \begin{array}{r} 86 \\ -35 \\ \hline \end{array} \quad \begin{array}{r} 98 \\ -45 \\ \hline \end{array} \quad \begin{array}{r} 82 \\ -41 \\ \hline \end{array} \quad \begin{array}{r} 76 \\ -33 \\ \hline \end{array}$$

$$\begin{array}{r} 85 \\ -21 \\ \hline \end{array} \quad \begin{array}{r} 99 \\ -52 \\ \hline \end{array}$$

FS109036 Subtraction

Answer Key

Page 2

5, 1, 4, 2, 3, 1;

3, 2, 2, 1, 4; 1;

2, 0, 3

Page 3

A CARTUNE!

4; 1, 0; 2, 5; 3, 6

Page 4

5, 3, 2; 4, 3, 3; 4, 2, 1; 4, 3, 0

Page 5

0, 1, 2;

3, 4, 5;

6, 0, 1;

2, 3, 5

Page 6

6 − 2 = 4, 5 − 1 = 4; 6 − 1 = 5,

3 − 2 = 1; 5 − 3 = 2, 6 − 5 = 1

Page 7

CABOOSE

Page 8

6, 1, 5, 2, 3, 4;

6, 2, 5, 3, 4

Page 9

A COLD MEDAL!

7, 5; 6, 1; 2, 4; 3, 0

Page 10

Page 11

Page 12

7 − 3 = 4, 7 − 4 = 3;

8 − 3 = 5, 4 − 3 = 1;

8 − 7 = 1, 8 − 7 = 1

Page 13

UMBRELLA

Page 14

7, 2, 6, 3, 4, 5;

8, 2, 7, 3, 6, 4, 5

Page 15

A STREET

4, 8; 3, 2; 6, 5; 7, 1

Page 16

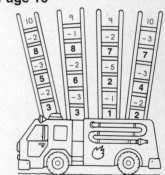

Page 17

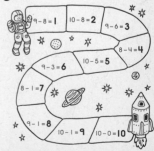